Jump-Starting Your Career:
A Practical Approach to the First Years of Teaching

Dr. Kimberly Ramadan
and
Dr. Michael White

Dedications

First and foremost, I want to dedicate this book to all teachers, new or veteran, who are working every day to meet the needs of the students in their classroom–you all are the true heroes.

To my family–my husband, Sherif, daughter Rylee Rose and son Ryan Edward–I want to thank you for your endless support and unwavering love in everything I do. I hope my kids learn through us that they can be and do anything they set their mind to. To my dad who is forever a cheerleader and is always willing to edit and revise anything I put in his path. Dad-I look up to your dedication to coaching and teaching for 40 years and hope that I have the opportunity to touch as many lives as you have. Finally, to my mom. She was taken from us far too soon but will always remain in our hearts. It is her drive and passion that guides me in my work and personal life. Mom–I know you are with us every day and I hope that I'm making you proud.

- Kim Ramadan

Here's hoping that one day soon the way we value things like teaching will not be based off of direct market contributions and considerations — that there will be a way we assign value to things different than the way we do now. It's wrong how much we undervalue the utterly core labor of keeping the human species going, learning and capable. We should place much greater value on care and teaching work. How we have to structure society to do that is an interesting question. But it is certainly not an impossible thing. It is simply a different thing.

Thanks to my valued family, Nikki, Chris and Dana, who care for and teach me, but had absolutely nothing to do with this book. And I wouldn't have it any other way!

- Mike White

Contributors

We would like to thank some special people who helped bring this book to life. They have added snippets along the way that tell the story of their experiences about various topics in the text. We hope that you will read their stories and feel their passion for what they do each and every day.

Ed Heintschel-Ed is a retired basketball coach after 40 years in the same school. He has devoted his life to his family, his basketball teams, and teaching English Language Arts for various grade levels. He is currently living his best retired life lakeside in Michigan.

Jenna Busam-Jenna is a talented author (check out her page "For the Love of Readers" on Facebook) and an amazing instructional coach. She is passionate about promoting reading at all ages and added a wonderful story to this book that is an example of growing relationships, but also a wonderful idea for building readers in your classroom!

Maghan Kirschner-Maghan is an exceptional instructional coach in North Carolina, leading hundreds of beginning teachers to be their best remarkable selves. She has teaching experience in Middle School Social Studies. Before becoming an instructional coach, Maghan has also had experience in administration.

Jessica Little-Jessica is a phenomenal 3rd grade teacher in Charlotte, North Carolina. She was an outstanding beginning teacher to coach because she is always willing to learn and grow. It is this growth mindset that has had a strong impact on her students' learning.

Patricia McRhoads-Patricia is an instructional coach in North Carolina. She has worn many hats in her career as an elementary school teacher, facilitator, administrator, and coach. She is always willing to try new things and has had great success with the teachers she coaches.

Dana Sanders-Dana is a mother, a wife, a daughter, a banker, and a reader/writer. She's great in all these roles.

About Us

Dr. Kimberly Ramadan is an instructional coach in Charlotte, North Carolina. She has had almost a decade of experience coaching beginning teachers in various schools and counties surrounding Charlotte. In her spare time, she loves boxing and spending time with her two kids (Rylee age 4 and Ryan age 8 months) and her husband, Sherif.

Dr. Michael White is a licensed pediatric psychologist. He has been the state chairperson of Ohio's School Psychology Association and more recently served three years as the assessment expert on Ohio's Department of Education's Academic Recovery Commission where he helped low performing schools. He is currently working with Southern Wesleyan University in the areas of curriculum and assessment.

Table of Contents

Introduction

Section 1 – Setting the Stage

    Chapter 1   Communicating with Adult Stakeholders

    Chapter 2   Students

Section 2 – The Plan

    Chapter 3   Routines and Procedures

    Chapter 4   Scheduling Time to Maximize Learning

    Chapter 5   Engagement

    Chapter 6   Data

    Chapter 7   Teaching is a Team Sport

    Chapter 8   Self-Care

Conclusion

Appendix A

Appendix B

References

Introduction

A world of high standards, international competition and public scrutiny presents teachers with significant challenges (Inman & Marlow, 2004). These challenges grow out of the promise our schools have made to deliver a world-class education, one that doesn't tolerate low level instruction or persistent gaps in student access to a quality education. The world is watching as we provide more complex instruction, covering a wider range of skills, to a diverse group of students, all while preparing students for jobs that are not yet created (Zhao, 2010). It is our response to these challenges that will determine the future for our students.

We have the opportunity to take education to a higher level and do something remarkable! It is through resilience when faced with a challenge that one becomes remarkable (Aguilar, 2018). Some people, when faced with a challenge, choose to run away, some remain but do nothing, while some choose to act. It's our hope that in some small way the following pages energize you to *act*.

This book was written to take some of the stress out of teaching by arming you with practical information and a method for making the best decisions for your students and yourself. It is filled with checklists, tips and ideas we hope you can take and use tomorrow in your classroom. The first section of the book sets the stage for teaching, by highlighting the importance of forming relationships with the adults in your teaching life (colleagues and parents) and with students.

We'll present some advice and examples for getting the most out of interactions with your colleagues, the parents/guardians, and most importantly your students. In the second part of the book, we shift the context from people to the plan. We'll take some enormously powerful teaching ideas and present them in a manner that can be used by anyone. For extra support, Appendix A contains an example of a lesson plan broken up into several tasks. These tasks also have assessment guides. Appendix B contains all of the checklists, tips and ideas that are mentioned throughout the book. Putting everything in one place, we hope, can be a reference guide for you as you continue your teaching career year after year.

Let's celebrate this new era in education and positively impact all students this school year!

SECTION 1 – SETTING THE STAGE

Chapter 1: Communicating with Adult Stakeholders

Research has shown that people skills and work relationships account for nearly three times as much success in any organization than technical skills (Goleman et. al., 2002). And the price tag for people avoiding malcontents, looking for and eventually leaving for other jobs can exceed $50,000 per employee per year across all jobs in the United States (Morse, 2005). One of the things that can drive people away from teaching are the relationships with others in or outside the building, such as colleagues, administration, parents, etc. In this chapter, we will discuss how to form, cultivate and grow relationships with adults.

Colleagues

I (Kim) entered teaching thinking that I would be placed on a harmonious team where everyone got along; we would work in unison to develop lesson plans for our kids, and we all would spend time together after school because we enjoyed each other that much. I was wrong. While it is important to get along with your colleagues, we are not expecting you to like every person you meet in your field. There are certainly personality conflicts that will occur each year. The trick is making sure that those feelings do not affect your work or the ability of people on each team to support one another.

Teaching, even though you are constantly surrounded by people, can be a lonely profession. Each teacher typically goes into their classroom for the majority of the day and stays within those four walls. While there are things like Professional Learning Communities (PLCs) and staff meetings where adults come together, they attribute to a small amount of time each week.

On top of that, some people in education (and in life) can be very negative. They harp on what students cannot do instead of what they are capable of achieving. To combat these issues, we suggest two things - find a person a positive person who you can talk to and avoid the "teacher lounge trap". First, while there may be negative people in the building, there are always some who believe strongly that all children can succeed, place a focus on student learning and their emotional health, and love what they do. Maybe not every day, but most days. Befriend this person. Pick up on energies that are positive. There are enough things that are draining about teaching, do not let other adults tax more emotional energy from you. Second, avoid the teacher lounge, or the copy room, or the classroom people go to complain. Nothing can be gained from gathering in a group complaining, and it also takes time away from being productive. Surrounding yourself with solution oriented encouraging people!

On your team, there is likely a group of different personalities. This is not a bad thing! In fact, it can be very positive to have a team with different talents and ideas. An interesting way to see what types of personalities are on teams is using a personality test such as Myers-Brigg or Enneagram Personality Types (see Figure 1). These tests allow you to see the different personality types on a team, people's individual strengths, and areas of growth. A strong team typically has a mix of several different personality types, which is what makes it strong. The more diversity on the team, the more teachers can learn from one another.

Personality Test Links

- Meyers-Briggs - https://www.16personalities.com/free-personality-test

- Enneagram - https://tests.enneagraminstitute.com/

Figure 1. Personality test links

In a strong school structure, one way that your colleagues will collaborate is through team meetings focused on student data and growth, often called Professional Learning Communities (PLCs), or data team meetings, or grade level meetings. These will be discussed in more detail in Chapter 7.

Parents/Guardians

Getting to know the parents or guardians of your students is as important as getting to know your students themselves; it is important to respect and address these stakeholders. Parents and guardians can be our greatest partners or biggest roadblocks in the day-to-day business of teaching their children. They, after all, know your students the best and, hopefully, have the same goals as you. It is of upmost importance to make sure, early in your relationship, they understand you have a shared vision – the success of their child. Second, it's important to note that we have never met a parent who did not have their child's best interest in mind. Parents are passionate about their children and there is no doubt they care deeply for their them. When either party (you or them) get frustrated, the key is helping parents understand that you, too, care about their child. The subsequent sections outline some tips you may find helpful.

Introductory Phone Call

The beginning of the year is hectic, but do not underestimate the importance of making positive contact with parents or guardians early. This phone call is ideally done before meeting the students for the first time but can be completed within the first couple weeks of school. It is important to remember this is a two-way conversation. It bears repeating, parents know their children best and hold information that could be helpful to you as a teacher. Below are some important tips about that first conversation:

- Before going into conversations with parents, be prepared with questions to ask, information you would like to share with them, and answers to typically asked questions

- Take notes as you talk with them (see Figure 2)

Questions for Parents/Guardians

- What do you feel is the most important thing for me to know about your child?

- Who are the important people in your child's life?

- How does your child learn best (lecture, hands-on, note-taking, movement, etc.)?

- What are some goals you have for your child?

- Is there anything else I need to know about your child?

Information You May Want to Share

**A word of caution first, do not share personal information with students, parents or guardians. There is a difference between telling a little about yourself to build relationships and oversharing. Check with a mentor or coach if you need support with these conversations.

- A little about yourself (we do not suggest you start off telling them this is your first-year teaching)

- Teaching style or philosophy

- What a typical day looks like for their child

- Discipline policy

- Communication (how best to get ahold of you and when you will respond) It is critical to establish mutual expectation around the type and frequency of communication.

Typically Asked Questions

- What is the policy on late work?

- How are differences in learning accommodated?

- What is the discipline policy?

- How will I know if my child is performing on grade level?

- Is there a gifted program and how does my child get into it?

- How can my child get extra help if they do not understand something?

- How can I help my child at home?

Figure 2 Questions and Information to Share with Parents

Date	Time	Placed by	Name of Parent	Child's Name & Reason for Call	Notes

Figure 3. Sample phone call record

Some parents or guardians have had bad experiences (or have heard of bad experiences from other parents) with your school, and they may want to share these during this conversation. Be very careful to listen, but do not feed into any bad conversations about your colleagues or your school. If you contact a parent or guardian who is angry about something that occurred the school last year or over the summer, let them know they can alert the principal or administrator in charge. Assure them this is a new school year, and you are committed to making it a great one!

Communication During the School Year

It is also important to continue communication with parents and guardians throughout the school year. As stated in the previous section, it is important to discuss with parents or guardians (1) what type of communication works best (phone call, email, etc.) and (2) when they can expect to hear from you. For example, it is not possible for you to answer parent phone calls while teaching, but it is plausible that parents can expect to hear back from you within 24 hours of their initial contact. Do make sure to keep a log when talking with parents (see Figure 3).

In addition to regular communication, there may be times when parents approach you about something that is bothering them. Below are some tips that we suggest if a parent is upset:

- First, remember, as stated above, almost all parents are coming from a place of love for their child.

- Allow the parent to voice their concern.

- Do not get into a situation where you are emailing back and forth with a parent. It is often better to discuss their concern in person, rather than through email or on the phone.

- If necessary, have a mentor, curriculum support person, assistant principal, or principal present when talking with the parent.

- When the parent expresses his or her concern, do not react emotionally; rather, take a deep breath, state the facts of the situation and allow those to lead the conversation.

- Come to the table with solutions for the issue.

- Leave the conversation with a plan to help their child that everyone can live with.

- Confirm understanding and acceptance. Ask them if they agree to the next step(s).

- Plan a follow up, whether through email, phone call or in person.

Classroom Newsletter

The typical, and quite frustrating, response when parents ask their child what they learned at school - "nothing." Classroom newsletters are a way to combat that issues. Newsletters are not only for kindergarten students; in fact, they are powerful tools for all grade levels. They allow teachers to reach parents, inform them of what's happening in the classroom, and get their support for activities. They are appropriate for all elementary grades and beyond. Parents know that children can be tight-lipped when it comes to sharing tidbits about the school day, and classroom newsletters fill in the gaps. Give parents a "conversation starter" in your newsletters, such as "Ask your child about Tuesday's floating egg experiment." In addition to student work and homework, newsletters can include:

- important upcoming events in the classroom and school

- dates to remember

- curriculum notes and current topics of study

- materials needed in the classroom or a wish list

- changes to class rules or policies

- details about field trips

- informational surveys

- messages of thanks for materials or to volunteers

- ideas to help parents support kids at home

- ways for parents to be involved (Parents have varying degrees of comfort in helping their students. Offer easy and concrete ways parents can support student success through everyday activities.)

- photos of recent activities

- congratulations to students for achievements

- requests for volunteer support (Have ways parents might be able to help from home if they cannot make it in the classroom - donating items, cut out items you might need, putting bags together of items students need to access for instruction, etc.)

There has been a shift from paper/pencil newsletters to electronic versions such as websites, Facebook, Twitter, etc. Online versions are often preferred over paper/pencil because of the convenience, speed and ease at which creating and receiving information can be. While this is true, be sure to check with your school or district about their online policies.

So far, we have discussed the importance of knowing and communicating with stakeholders in and outside of the building. The next chapter will focus on the most important people you encounter each day – the students. We will discuss how to get to know your students and how to keep them engaged throughout the school year.

Chapter 2: Students

The first day of school, even for veteran teachers, is like a blind date. Teachers arrive with anticipation, nervous and wanting to impress their students. No one, not a teacher or a student, returns to the same school they left last year. Mr. Harms might be a 28-year veteran of seventh grade math, but this year there's a new assistant principal, a new teacher on the team, and slightly different standards. Mr. Harms has new people to work with, and a new curriculum to learn. He, too, may feel like a brand-new teacher this year. Not only that, he has a fresh, exciting new group of students with whom to work.

What's your first order of business? Put aside teaching standard 4.01 for a moment and work on classroom culture. Building relationships is important, and we will discuss how to do that in this chapter; but, above all, students need to feel *safe* when they walk into your room each and every day (Rogers, 2013). By safe, we are not referring to having a lock on the door to keep intruders out. Rather we mean that students should feel like they are free to be themselves, and are provided choice in your classroom, are able to make mistakes and not be judged, and that they have something to contribute to the culture of the classroom. This is no easy task, but it is extremely important for a positive climate.

In the beginning of the year, concentrate on getting to know your students, building relationships with them, creating a classroom culture, setting routines and expectations and allowing students getting to know each other and students getting to know themselves. The time spent collecting this data and building this climate of rapport and relationships will pay dividends throughout the year.

The more you know about your students' background knowledge, interests and culture, the better your relationship, classroom management and instruction will be. Just how critical is this information? Robert Marzano, one of the foremost educational researchers believes "the quality of relationships teachers have with students is the keystone of effective management and perhaps even the entirety of teaching" (Marzano, 2007). There are many ways to get to know your students. The next sections will focus on some strategies for building relationships.

Community

One year, a principal had her staff climb aboard a school bus for a tour of the neighborhood where their students live. The principal acted as tour guide, pointing out clues to the community and its families, pointing out places of interest like the location of churches known to be active in the surrounding neighborhoods and the large number of apartment complexes. Touring the students' neighborhoods can be very powerful, but remember it is only a piece of what you learn about the students in your classroom.

Interests

It's imperative that you know what your students like, so you can begin building relationships with them. There are many ways to do this, but one idea includes interviewing or using a questionnaire (some Figure 4). Both your questionnaire and interview should elicit a variety of data to confirm the basic information you have about where students live, and help you form a more complete picture of each student. Ask students how they learn best. Read these interviews to plan engaging lessons that reach your students and allow the answers to begin conversations.

Student questionnaires

- Beginning of Year Questionnaire:

  https://pernillesripp.com/2013/07/23/my-student-questionnaire-for-beginning-of-year/

- First day of school questionnaire:

  https://www.csun.edu/science/ref/management/student-questionnaire/student-questionnaires.html

- What Kids Can Do Questionnaire:

  http://www.whatkidscando.org/specialcollections/student_voice/pdf/Who%20Are%20You%20Questionnaire.PDF

Figure 4. Student questionnaire links

Students may share data about siblings and extended family members who might live with them. You can learn how they spend their time outside of school. For example, do they take care of themselves or other siblings after school? Are they on a sport team or other after-school activities? Do they have a job after school? The survey can even reveal how they interact with and view other members of the class. You also want to learn what your students' value. Asking questions about whom and what they admire can provide insight into their cultural norms.

There are many creative ways to have students complete an interest survey or questionnaire. Rather than passing out #2 pencils on the first day of school, requiring students to use their best handwriting, and quietly complete survey questions, have students express themselves creatively. Some ideas might include:

- Consider giving each student a small journal and some old magazines and see what they value. They can paste pictures of their interests and date that page. They can add to the journal as their interests grow and evolve throughout the year.
- Have students interview one another and introduce themselves to you.
- Allow students make an "Identity Portrait", where they draw a picture of their face and in and around it they draw or write things they identify with.
- Have students bring in pictures of people that are important to them.
- Have them write poetry or songs.

Recently, a teacher took it a little further. Karen Lowe, a Middle School teacher in Oklahoma, had her students write down something that was bothering them or weighing heavy on their hearts (Lamb, 2019). She then asked them to crumple up their piece of paper and throw it across the room. Students then picked up a paper, opened it, and read it aloud. The student who wrote the original story could choose to expand on it, or not, it was their choice. Karen said what happened next was incredible. Students opened up about dealing with cancer, death of family members and pets, suicide, and family members in prison. The stories that were told left everyone in tears. Karen then placed all of the crumpled paper in a plastic bag by the door of her classroom to remind the students, and herself, that they all have baggage they are dealing with, and they are all loved.

No matter which activity you choose, it is important to model the activity by participating along with your students. Giving students some information about yourself (what you value, care about, and like to do) will allow students to feel closer to you and, thus, might help them trust you a bit more. A word of caution – do not go too far with this. There is a line that you must draw in terms of the amount of information students know about you. If there is any question, be sure to contact your mentor or coach for advice on what or not to share with your students.

Students' interests can quickly change throughout the year, so we suggest spending a few minutes every day with students talking about what they care about inside and outside of school. Think of this as taking their temperature. You will be amazed at the wealth of unconventional and valuable information you can gain from brief Morning Meetings. Purposeful collection of

23

student interests doesn't just help you to form relationships, it helps you to develop lessons and units that are more engaging for students.

Building Relationships: A Basketball Coaches Perspective
I have recently retired from 45 years of coaching and teaching (one and the same). It took me a little while to figure out that the key to success in these fields is inspiring those you coach and teach, not simply being demanding. In effect, you have to build relationships. The key to any relationship (personal, professional, others) is trust. So, key to coaching or teaching is developing the trust so kids know you care about them as people, beyond players or students. Develop that trust, and the kids will try to do what you ask at the optimal level for their respective abilities.

There is one specific kid who has stuck with me after all these years. I once coached a young man named Nathan. He was an inner-city kid coming to a somewhat diversified but predominantly white all-male Catholic college prep school, quite a change from his previous school environment. I am certain that he had had limited contact with white people and now he faced this pronounced change.

There are pressures on African American kids to do well in sports, especially basketball because African Americans dominate the sport at its highest levels. Add to that, he had considerable pressure from his parents. Because he was a very good player, I demanded a lot from Nathan but rarely did I yell or get emotional with him. When correction was necessary, I would pull him aside and quietly talk to him. Frequently, I would follow up with conversation prior to the next practice. In his senior year, he was player of the year in our League and led his team to the State tournament Final 4. With careful work on our interaction, he trusted me and he and his team truly maxed out their potential.

Morning Meetings

Morning meetings can be done the first 10-15 minutes of class each day. They are typically discussions and students meet in a circle on the carpet or in desks. These meetings can include:

- Get to know you activities

- Exciting things that happened the night/day before

- Content or data review

- Energizers

- Reminders for the day

- Meditation

Morning meetings offer students choices when it comes to the way they communicate their interests, talents and personal information. Students who might struggle to write about these things will often be able to talk passionately about them, draw or describe them to you in a one-on-one conversation. These meetings also allow students to learn about their classmates as the discussion unfolds. It gives you a sense for where students are emotionally before the day starts, and helps you form relationships with them from the beginning of the year.

10 by 2 Rule

There are times that creating relationships with some students is tougher than others. For some kids, the questionnaires and morning meeting will not be enough to form a relationship with them. They will meet your attempts to get to know them with a brick wall. These are the students who, beyond a doubt, forming relationships is the most important. They are the students who might need you in their life more than others. It takes time, but it's worth it.

The 10 by 2 strategy is fairly simple to implement. For 10 school days consecutively, for 2 minutes each day, talk to this student about whatever he or she wants. This is not your agenda to find out more about them, but rather their chance to just talk. Your job is to openly listen. If they want to talk about football, you talk about football. If they want to talk about the latest video game, that's what you talk about (research it later if you have no idea what it is). By the end of the 10 days, the idea is that student has softened just a bit and you are able to work on building a relationship from there.

Academics

Researching students' prior academic performance can also give you information about them. Data is available about students' prior performance on standardized tests and other assessments. While this is only one piece of data, it can be valuable in helping you understand the academic history of your students. By law, as a classroom teacher, you need to know if there are students in your class who have an individualized educational plan (IEP) in place. If so, review the plan to determine how special services will be delivered. Will the student report to a resource room for part of the day, or will the teacher be with you in your room? Some ideas for knowing how your students have performed academically:

- Review student cumulative records to gather data about your students as learners. Look at all academic records.

- Analyze state test data to identify strengths and weaknesses in individual students and the class as a whole.

- Ask to see a copy of your school's state report card and find out if your state offers on-line reports such as item analyses and individual student reports.

- Look for a folder containing an Individualized Educational Plan (IEP).

- Make an appointment with the special education teacher in your building to review the IEP goals of your students and discuss how you will work together to help them achieve these goals.

- Check other assessment platforms your school might have for past data. Some schools have running records in reading or other early literacy assessments on each student.

If you need help finding these documents or reading them once you have them, talk to your mentor or someone in the building for help.

High Expectations

There will be a day, and likely several, where the excitement of a new job wears off and when you will think teaching students to master a certain math or reading standard is impossible. You may even fantasize about alternate career opportunities in hotel/motel management, and ask yourself, *Will I ever feel like I'm not drowning? Can I really make a difference? Are my students going to grow? Can I meet the academic expectations, but also the social and emotional needs of all of my students? Am I doing enough?*

Perhaps many of your students come to school carrying the weight of the world on their shoulders. There may be things they are dealing with at home that you cannot even comprehend. Perhaps they speak a different language or have learning challenges. Perhaps they live in a constant state of trauma, and are struggling to get through the day, let alone pay attention and work hard. Is it fair to have high expectations of them and you?

You don't have to look hard to find research which supports the notion that some children are destined to fail. In 1966, Professor James S. Coleman published a congressionally mandated study on why schoolchildren in minority neighborhoods performed at far lower levels than children in suburban areas. Titled *Equality of Educational Opportunity*, his mammoth, 737-page study reached the unsettling conclusions that teachers and schools were not society's great equalizers after all and that the main cause of the achievement gap was in the backgrounds and resources of families (Coleman et al., 1966).

Teachers, and at times entire school districts, can get caught up in the thesis that certain children can't achieve at high levels. You may even shockingly hear people refer to students we are describing as "these kids", for example, "'these kids' cannot grow," "I don't know what to do with 'these kids'". "'They' are not capable of sitting still, so why make them?" Some researchers spend endless hours excusing, tracking and correlating the percent of low-birth weight babies, percent of children born to single moms, percent of children from families who receive government assistance, and percent of children with disabilities. Armed with printouts, statistics and newspaper clippings, researchers will lament that, it is "too hard" to grow students who come from economically disadvantaged areas. And then some teachers start settling for "good enough" work. The result is some members of the school system do not expect very much from themselves or their students – and in turn do not get much from the students.

For many educators and policy makers, research like the Coleman Report study raised a haunting proposition: Outside forces tug so hard that they cannot be overcome by any particular kind of school, any set of in-school reforms or an effective and caring teacher. What if schools and teachers were not the answer?

We argue this report cannot define children or their abilities. Before throwing your hands up and exclaiming, "There's nothing I can do," consider the progress that has been made with students who had the odds stacked against them. In the fall of 1998, the Education Trust identified 1,200 high achievement schools, with poverty levels over 50 percent. Katie Haycock found six characteristics that were common to all High Poverty-High Achievement Schools.
These characteristics were:

(1) use of state standards extensively to design curriculum and instruction, assess student work, and evaluate teachers;

(2) increased instructional time in reading and mathematics to help students meet standards;

(3) large proportion of funds devoted to support professional development focused on changing instructional practice;

(4) implementation of comprehensive systems to monitor individual student progress and provide extra support to students as soon as it is needed;

(5) focused efforts to involve parents in helping students meet standards;

(6) had state and district accountability systems in place

Haycock continues energizing educators with reports of "High Achievement-High Poverty" schools. (If interested, check out several excellent reports at https://edtrust.org/dispelling_the_myth/)

Psychologically, we can think of few things more terrifying than choosing or staying in a profession that has no impact or chance of changing a student's life. We are teachers, not potted plants. Students don't march past us year after year without having us touch their hearts and minds and vice versa. Intuitively, you know this is true. Thus, we must rise above the narrative that students are not able to succeed and do better for them. They are counting on us not to fail.

Mistakes of the Heart

Some teachers reject the notion of high failure rates for poor students but make a mistake of the heart. In these classes students pass because they are given credit for attendance or for being non-disruptive and polite. These students will receive A's and B's for C -- or worse, D – work. Their teacher will inflate scores based on effort or the lack of support at home. Teachers will accept assignments from students any day of the year with any excuse. Justifications are made for some students and, while some of what students are going through is heart wrenching, students are not going to succeed without being held to high expectations. This is true for **all** students.

Teachers may think they are "protecting" children by not telling the students and parents the truth. That truth is: *You are behind your classmates, and we will all have to work harder, longer*

30

and smarter to catch you up. This will probably require more effort than that of some of your classmates so we will have to support each other along the way. But catching up is so important that we have to do whatever it takes. I believe you can do it, and I will help you in any way I can.

Figure 3 provides a checklist summarizing ways to get to know your students.

Ideas for Getting to Know your Students

- Tour the neighborhood they live in

- Develop/borrow a questionnaire (see examples in this chapter)

- Have students bring pictures (or draw pictures) of people that are important to them

- Have students create connections to each other by sitting in a circle and saying one thing that is unique about them. If someone connects with that in some way, they throw a ball of yarn to that person. When they are done, they see the web they have created that shows the connections they have to each other.

- Have students create an inner circle and outer circle. Ask a question to the students and have them each answer, then the inside circle rotates, and another question is asked.

- Take time to know how to spell and pronounce each child's name correctly.

- Implement a short morning meeting into your schedule each morning.

> - Take time to review their cumulative folders at the beginning of each school year.

Figure 5. Checklist of ways to get to know your students

We want to leave chapter 2 with a story about how to build relationships with your students, while also fostering a love of reading.

〰〰〰〰〰〰〰〰〰〰〰〰〰〰〰〰〰〰〰〰〰〰〰〰

Book Tastings

As a reading specialist I watched a group of students be pulled out of their classrooms repeatedly for extra test prep, additional remediation groups, and re-administrations of the standardized end-of-grade test. They were quickly labeled "bad at reading" if not in the minds of their observant peers, then by themselves. I wanted to find a way to honor this group of students and re-engage them as readers. Afterall, who could blame this group of students for hating reading at this point?

We received a donation from a generous high school partner who raised money so I could purchase high interest-low readability books. This group of 4th graders participated in a Book Tasting featuring the brand-new books before adding them to the school media center. They got dibs on all the new books!

In order to elevate the experience and maximize engagement, I delivered invitations before the event and posted a sign in the hall advertising the Book Tasting to come. On the day of the Book Tasting, I draped a tablecloth over each table group and set the tables with placemats, battery-operated candles, and most importantly stacks of beautiful, brand-new books.

Students found the seat with their name place card, yet another way to make the event feel extra special. During the Book Tasting they read short experts from books of their choice and shared

them with the other readers at their tables. After the final round of tasting, students indicated which books they wanted to read and wrote a reflection.

The written reflections confirmed the power of the Book Tasting to re-engage this group of readers. Student after student commented on how much they loved the event because they got to read books they never thought they would like, how much fun they had reading the books, and how excited they were to check out these new books from the media center. One student wrote, "We got to read books. It was fun." It doesn't get much better than that.

~~~~~~

Section 2 – The Plan

Chapter 3: Routines and Procedures

Anyone who has children or spent a day in a classroom knows that most humans, students included, are creatures of habit. They take comfort in the expected, and they will bring to your attention any deviation from tradition. Having set routines for lunch count, storing materials, entering the classroom in the morning, coming and going as a class, distributing papers, collecting homework, etc., saves time. The list below, while not comprehensive, gives you an idea of what may require a routine. It is essential in the beginning of the year to teach and practice these routines with your students (see Figure 6). In addition, create team captains to help minimize the number of students moving at one time. All children should be involved as much as possible in maintaining the smooth operation of the classroom.

Things that may need a routine:

- Getting students attention (attention getter)

- Entry Routine (when students enter classroom)

  - Where to sit

  - What to unpack

  - Where to put coat, book bag, homework

  - What to do when done unpacking (bell ringer)

- Transitions

  - Tables to carpet

  - Carpet to tables

- Tables to line up

- Carpet to line up

- Outside the classroom to desks

- Outside the classroom to carpet

- Attendance

- Lunch count

- Materials (how to get and how to put away)

- Distributing papers

- Collecting homework

- Collecting in class work

- What to do when finished with an assignment

- Sharpening pencils

- Getting a tissue

- Getting technology such as iPads or chrome books

- Rotating during centers (practice each rotation without actually having students do work)

Figure 6. Checklist of routines

Routines do not turn into procedures until they are practiced repeatedly. Every single routine that is important for the function of the classroom needs to have a plan created by the teacher and needs to be modeled and practiced over and over to exhaustion by students until it becomes a procedure. This may be the single most important activity, aside from creating relationships with students, to ensure that your classroom functions well.

It takes time to develop a plan for a routine. But, trust us, it's worth it. In the beginning of the year, we suggest sitting in the classroom, perhaps during workdays or before, and physically imagine being the students in order to develop a routine. When planning this, sit in the student's chair and walk through the routine as if you a student. Imagine what issues might come up, or steps you may have missed.

When talking to teachers, they indicate arrival and dismissal are points of stress. This is often because these events are not planned out or practiced. Sometimes, teachers forget to not only tell students where they want them to put their things, but they also have to practice it with them, even in high school. We cannot assume that because a student is 16, he or she does not need to be taught organizational skills, especially because the way you want your classroom run might be very different from the person across the hall! It is essential to think through each step of the entry routine, or any routine, in order to make sure there is no question as to the expectation. See Figure 7 for an example of a routine for entering the classroom.

Routine: Entering the classroom

We suggest this be practiced on the first (and maybe even second and third) day of school. On the first day, students have not practiced this yet, so they might just go to their seats when they arrive. Have something for them to do while waiting for everyone to get there. Then, after everyone has come in, have them get all of their belongings as if they are just arriving for the day and practice the routine.

What it will look like: Students stagger in during arrival in the morning. The teacher will stand at the door where he or she can see inside the classroom as well as the hallway, greeting each student as he or she arrives. As students enter, they will take their book bags to their seat, unpack any items they need (book, agendas, homework, notebook) and hang up their book bags and coats. They will turn in their homework in their bin and begin "Do Now", which will be written on the board. The directions for morning routine will also be written on the board.

What teacher will say: As each student enters, the teacher will say "Good morning, come in silently, unpack your items at your desk, hang up your book bag, and begin your Do Now"

> **How students will practice:**
>
> - Line up at the door outside with all items
>
> - Greet teacher
>
> - Go to desk and unpack all items
>
> - Turn in homework
>
> - Begin "Do Now"
>
>
> Students will practice this multiple time. Each time, leaving the room with their book bags and acting as if they are arriving that day.

Figure 7 Example of a Routine

Practice should occur within the first weeks of school and be reinforced throughout the year. Keep in mind that some routines can be taught during instruction. For example, passing out papers can be done during independent work, rather than in isolation. It would be a good idea to review all routines and procedures when coming back from a long break.

There are times, despite careful planning, that a routine or procedure was not developed at the beginning of the year as it should. Do not fear – routines can be developed at any time throughout the year. What we often ask our teachers during the school year is – "what is driving you nuts about student behavior?" Often times it is something like "students are talking too much during instructional times" or "when they leave my class at the end of the period (or day), they are so loud". When we ask what routine has been established for these periods of annoyance, almost always the answer is none. Then, we focus on establishing a routine and the problem is fixed! It is never too late to develop a routine or procedure for a classroom.

Tips and Tricks for Developing Routines:

- Develop a plan for routines

- If possible, physically sit in students' seat or walk around the area you are planning

- Practice the plan over and over until students are able to master without any errors

- Review after long breaks

- Utilize table or class helpers to speed up routines

- When student behavior is getting under your skin, ask yourself if you have a routine and if you have practiced it enough with the class

- Make anchor charts of important routines and post around the classroom at the beginning of the year

- Practice what not to do to avoid common mistakes

Next, we will discuss how to organize your time to increase learning.

Chapter 4: Scheduling Time to Maximize Learning

Whether organization comes naturally to you or not, it is extremely important to organize yourself throughout the school year. The reality is the time you have to teach may not be as much as you think! Consider a full calendar year – 365 days. Now, subtract summer vacation which is about 86 days. Next, subtract weekends and holidays, about 96 more days. Let's not forget professional development days, early dismissal, parent conferences, snow days, fog days and "someone smelled gas" days. They eat up about 12 days. There are also class field trips, picnics, Thanksgiving parties, holiday wrapping day, Kwanza, Hanukkah, awards assembly and concerts. Maybe that's another deduction of 10 days. Oh, we almost forgot, you still have to deduct your state's testing days – that's 10 more.

What starts out looking like gobs of time is quickly whittled down (see the Figure 8). You and your students are eventually left with about 150 days to teach and learn. Assuming you spend an hour a day on reading instruction, that equals about 19 eight-hour days. Think how little you learned on your job the first 19 days.

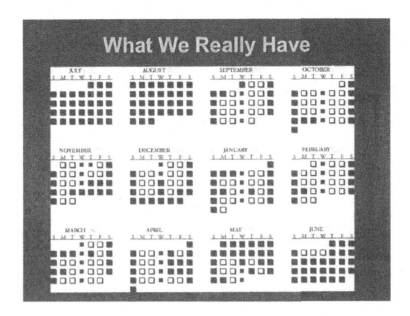

Figure 8. A calendar of what the year might look like after all of the days off and special events are considered. The white squares represent days where teaching takes place.

"Timewasters"

Once you realize the actual amount of time that you will have to teach, it becomes clear that you and your students can't afford to waste a minute. It is up to you to identify the things that take time away from learning and eliminate them. This list is different for every teacher, but the list below provides some possible areas that might be "timewasters":

- Transitions from or to lunch, specials, bathroom

- Transitions inside the classroom (i.e. passing out papers, sharpening pencils)

- Beginning of class

- End of class

- Prepping materials for the day (pulling up slide shows, getting materials for the students, etc.)

42

- Time in between activities in class

If you find yourself spending more than seconds on transitions (depending on the grade) or feel like you do not have rules set in place, then you may want to return to Chapter 3 and tighten up routines. The rest of this chapter contains additional ideas for making sure that time is maximized.

Schedule

One of the first things to establish well before students walk in the door is your daily schedule. You will need a schedule that considers all part of your day or block and is posted for everyone to see. You can alter a schedule to work better (with permission from administration as needed) but first you have to have one. Some things to put on your calendar will be provided by the school (lunch, specials, block times if you are in upper grade/middle or high school), and others will be by your design, depending on your school. Chart your schedule, hang it near a clock, and stick to it. But also, be open to adjusting if something is not working. Some things to consider when making a schedule:

- Chunk blocks of time so you are not doing direct instruction for long periods of time, no matter what the grade level. (Tip: One thing I tell my teachers is take a student's age and add one. That is usually how long they can be sitting in one task)
- Consider transition times to and from periods, and in between activities. This time should not be long. Even young students can move from one place to another in seconds, especially if the teacher is counting down. This will a game and is fun for them.

- While it doesn't need to be posted, develop a plan for your planning time. Some time will be devoted to grade level meetings but be sure to have a plan for "free" planning times to maximize your productivity.

Calendar

A calendar will help you keep on pace and make sure you are covering all the standards in the year. There are several calendars to consider.

Pacing Calendar

There are times where we have seen teachers get to the end of the year and they are panicked because they have not taught all of their standards and the end of year test is looming. That's why it is important to have a pacing calendar. This can be simply a calendar of the school year, with standards written out so you know when you are teaching what standard and when. This can be adjusted slightly as the year goes on, and you need to make changes or allow more time, but again, be cautious about making sure to teach all material. See the suggested steps before for how to develop a pacing calendar:

- Know your standards. Typically, these can be found online, in school documents or ask your mentor.
- Consider when your final assessments are, whether the students are taking end of course or end of year assessments. These are determined by the county, district or school.

- Give yourself some review days (maybe a week or so depending on the course) before the final assessment.

- Consider the order you want to teach standards. For example, you may have quarterly assessments where you need to cover a certain number of standards. You would then want to make sure all of those standards are taught before the assessment. Differently, you may have standards that build upon one another, so they make sense to be taught in a certain order.

- Finally, calendar out your standards, and make sure there are no standards missing.

Planning Units

Once your pacing has been established, you can then focus on planning units. When planning units, it might help to follow these steps:

- First, think about your unit assessment. What standards do students need to know? How are you going to assess them? Create your assessment, schedule your assessment day, and perhaps a review day before the assessment.

- Then, how much time will you need for each standard? Consider how you are going to teach each standard and how much time you will need. Standards are typically complex and have multiple parts that need to be broken up. How will you break those up into lessons and how many days will you need?

- Finally, plan each day. Think about how your block will be broken up and how you will teach students something, but also have them practice.

- Reflection is also important. On your day-to-day calendar, choose one with space to record ideas for reflection and improving yesterday's lesson.

- Also, on your day-to-day calendar, record school-wide events, test days, appointments with school personal, and other personal appointments, and anything else that you need to remember. Make a habit of checking your calendar each day as often as is appropriate.

Consider providing your students (and their parents) with their own monthly calendars that contain instructional themes for the month, assignments, quizzes, tests, special events, etc. If students are old enough to manage their calendars independently, you can let them track this information for themselves. Students can staple the calendars to the inside covers of their notebooks for quick reference. Your calendar will visually map the teaching time that will be open to you and what you plan to do with it over the course of each month.

Planning for Absences

Nothing is worse than waking up with a 102-degree fever, knowing you need to stay home, only to have no plan for your students. It is best to consider, while you are well and able to plan for it, an idea for what will happen when you are not in class and a substitute teacher must handle it. A time with a substitute should still be a day where learning happens. At the beginning of the school year, and then after each quarter or semester from there, develop a substitute teacher binder or folder. Below are some tips for preparing for a substitute folder:

- Provide detailed lesson plans for the sub. Fill your substitute folder with meaningful activities that can be done at any time during the year. For example, a Time for Kids magazine with a lesson to practice determining importance within non-fiction text, or a math and science graphing activity involving classroom materials that are always on hand.

- Make sure your sub knows how to log into your computer and other technology devices. Often, schools will provide a substitute login. Do not give substitutes your log in, as they may be able to access personal or sensitive information.

- Have a folder with a seating chart and explanation of classroom procedures. Provide enough detail about procedures so the substitute can flawlessly run the class, including transitions, how students get and organize materials, where they turn in materials, etc.

- Designate a colleague who knows your classroom to be a backup for unforeseen circumstances and offer to do the same for him or her. Provide the name of this colleague to your sub as well as how they can help.

- Also provide names of student assistants who can support the sub in the classroom.

- In the beginning of the year, explain your expectations for students' appropriate interaction with a substitute. Then, if you know you will be absent, remind them again.

Your "Stop Doing" List

When your job starts to feel completely overwhelming and it seems like you could work 24 hours a day and still not be done with anything, chances are you have put teaching before yourself (more on this in the last chapter on self-care). You've allowed so many tasks to pile up on your plate that they all seem equally important, and it feels like the world will come crashing down if you don't complete them all.

If you're not sure whether a task is important, ask yourself, what would happen if I didn't do this? For example, what would the consequence be for not rewriting every misspelled word on every student's paper? How would your lesson go if the worksheet you create doesn't have adorable clip art? What would be the result of not color-coding your filing system, creating a lengthy welcome packet for your student teacher, or changing your bulletin board borders on a weekly basis? Does *every* thing your students do need to be graded? Assemblies, announcements, cutting, coloring, pasting, dittos and other projects-without-purpose can take on a life of their own. Try this 15-minute drill by yourself or at a staff meeting to develop a stop doing list.

On a paper, create the table below

- List all of the initiatives adopted over the last five years (or however long you've been teaching) by the county, district or school.

- Cross out those that have been evaluated and eliminated because they were not working or not related to standards, or goals.

Initiatives/Activities Started in the Last 2 Years	Initiatives/Activities Reviewed and Terminated

What we have found, in most schools, the staff members discover that they rarely *stop doing* anything. They simply throw new initiatives on the initiative cart that they are already pulling behind them. Try the same activity yourself, with your classroom initiatives. And if you are a new teacher and don't need a *stop-doing* list, create a *don't-even-think-about-it* list!

Chapter 5: Engagement

Now that you have decided and scheduled what to teach, it's time to think about how to teach.

The good news: nearly thirty-five years of research provide the ingredients of effective teaching.

Some great resources to have on your bookshelf include:

- *Making Standards Work* by Douglas Reeves

- *Teach Like Your Hair's on Fire* by Rafe Esquith

- *The Art & Science of Teaching* by Robert Marzano

- *The First Days of School* by Harry Wong and Rosemary Wong

- *Results Now* by Mike Schmoker

- *The Schools Our Children Deserve* by Alfie Kohn

One of the most surprising messages from the research on teaching is that high achievement is usually a by-product of one important thing: Engagement! Remember all the student interest data you collected in chapter 3? Here's where you'll use it!

Emotional Engagement

In his landmark book, *The Schools Our Children Deserve,* Alfie Kohn (1999) warned us, the that the most pressing issue teachers is student disengagement. The same rules that apply to the school playground apply to the classroom: Children do not work or play well with others they don't like, and they don't keep playing a game in which they always lose. In other words, your students will be engaged as long as the material is relevant, as long as they think someone cares and is there to help, and as long as they believe there is a chance that they will be successful.

Think back to your days as an elementary or middle school student. Who were your best teachers? They may have shaved their heads, kissed a pig for fundraisers or slept on the roof of the school building roof if every student read twenty books. But, more importantly, they proved that they were willing to go the distance to engage you and make you feel that they had a personal stake in your success. Even when you weren't excited about an assignment or a chapter in the book, that wasn't as important as the attitude you had toward the teacher and the class. Read the story below about the importance of building a relationship with students, even of other's tell you it's not worth it.

~~~~~~

Devin "Sunshine" Knott
I remember entering my 3rd year of teaching middle school in total fear, as I did every year. Fear that I was not going to have the same classroom management as the year before, fear that I wasn't going to be able to reach all of my kids in the way I had before. Overall fear that I was inadequate. Prior to the year beginning we received a roster of our homeroom students. These names were not unfamiliar to me. I made it a point to use my planning periods at the end of the previous year to go to the 7th grade hall and build relationships with the rising 8th graders. I remember placing a star next to the students names I knew when a colleague walked passed. "Ohhh. You have a tough homeroom. Let me see the list" and quickly ripped it out of my hands. Inside I cringed. I don't want to know what you think of my kids, I want to get to know them myself. Instead of politely asking her not to tell me about the experiences she has had she gave me feedback I will never forget. Feedback that motivated me to be different. "Ok. Well good luck with this one. Devin doesn't work. Don't make him. Let him sleep in the back of your class. I am not sure he even knows how to write a paragraph." cringed. This poor kid. What has his educational journey been like that causes people to speak about him in this way? As the year approached, I received the same feedback from other colleagues and even administrators. "He won't tear up your class, just don't expect much."

August 25, 2009. I met Devin. He was 6'3 with an overwhelming presence and a stoic look. Devin didn't smile at anyone on his journey down the hall, not teachers, not his friends. No one. He walked down the hall and you could see adults turn away from him. I felt a fear creep inside of me. Not a fear of Devin; but of being inadequate. How do I break down the negative perception of Devin? How do I undo the years of terrible educational experiences he has had? As he approached my door and tried to walk in. I stopped him and asked him to come back out. I asked him to tell me his name, which he mumbled under his breath and I said, "Nice to meet you Devin, I am Ms. C. I look forward to having you in my room." I spent the first month working on building a relationship with Devin any chance that I got. I would sit with him at lunch and talk about what he liked to do. I would find him when he was asked to leave other classes and bring him into mine. Slowly we built a relationship that has impacted me beyond words. We had our ups and downs but my expectation for Devin never changed. I commonly said to him "Once you cross that threshold, this is a new opportunity. I don't care what happened 5 years ago, 2 months ago or in your last block. You are here and you are here to learn." And he did just that. I met him where he was and worked tirelessly to build him up. He even graciously, allowed me to call him Sunshine in front of his peers. I distinctly remember the shock that overcame an administrator's face when they walked into my room in the middle of the lesson and Devin was working. Not just working but volunteering to answer questions. The shock increased when I said, "two claps for Sunshine on 3." and the same administrator who told me "just don't expect much" realized that "Sunshine" was Devin. The kid everyone was afraid of. The kid everyone held the lowest of expectations for. Devin changed that year, simply because someone believed he could. To this day we are in contact. He is now 24 and working on a music career. And yes, I still call him Sunshine in public and in front of his followers on social media. All because I believed.

~~~~~~

We all hope to develop relationships like the teacher, and my good friend, above. Here are some suggestions for fostering emotional engagement with your students:

- Meet students at the door in the morning. Genuinely be interested about their evening, morning, etc.

- Take pictures of the students working and display them.

- Use humor but not sarcasm

- Use words, songs, or dances from students' lives. Teach them about these things from your life as well.

- Volunteer to serve as a sponsor, advisor or chaperone to after-school clubs, organizations and events.

- Compliment students on what they are wearing.

- Make a point of watching at least one television program that your students watch.

- Be aware of video games they are playing and their music and Internet culture.

Rita Pierson gave an amazing Ted Talk in 2014. One of the things she noted was "you will not like every child you teach, but they can never, ever know it". Listen to her Ted Talk listed here https://www.ted.com/talks/rita_pierson_every_kid_needs_a_champion?language=en.

Engaging Scenarios

Teachers who are most successful in engaging students develop activities with students' interests in mind (Marzano, 2007). Try to create units and assignments that relate to student lives, are fun and awaken their curiosity. The information gleaned from parents, surveys and your morning meetings should provide you a treasure trove of material to work with.

Dave Burgess (2012), in his book, *Teach Like a Pirate* suggests using engaging scenarios or hooks to introduce your units. Rather than starting with "Today we are going to learn how to determine the area of a rectangle," hold up a contract signed by the iconic pop star of the week. Pretend, with the class, that she is coming to give a concert, and her contract demands that the stage be one hundred square feet, with security rope around three sides. Your class spends the rest of the morning working in small groups designing stages and computing how much rope they will need.

How about instruction that can be applied in real life? Most students are eager to do "grown-up things." Why not use their desire to act "grown-up" to teach? What do grown-ups read? When do grown-ups use math? Older students might be hooked into reading or doing math by reading and discussing *USA Today* or helping you balance a checkbook. Showing students how a classroom activity is related to the world of work or money are sure bets to get their attention. The lists below show some engaging scenarios you might use to introduce your instruction.

Elementary

- You've been asked to design a new Nintendo Game…

- You are on the committee to help our principal revise spirit week with new themes…

- As crime scene investigators, we need determine who borrowed our…

- Develop a movie script that is about searching for…

- A famous author wants you to write a different ending to his/her book…

Middle School

- Your community is considering a teen curfew. Write a letter to the editor of the local newspaper…

- Some of the surrounding schools are switching to a school uniform policy…

- Design a game that teaches young students…

- Make a timeline that shows the history of…

- Develop a song lyric that describes your…

High School

- As a member of the Senate, make the case for or against allowing kids to vote at seventeen…

- You are trying to help your older brother decide if it's better to rent or buy a house…

- Write a report that describes working with…

- Draw a picture that will get students interested in…

- Develop a concept map that will help your classmates…

Menus Not Mandates

Another way to academically engage students is to provide them with choices, a menu of tasks rather than a single task. Menus allow students a degree of control over learning and allow you to offer challenging, but achievable tasks to all your students regardless of their proficiency level. Let's imagine that you wanted to teach the following standard: *Describe and give examples of ways in which people interact with their physical environment, including use of land, location of communities, and design of shelters.* Rather than requiring everyone to create a Venn diagram to compare and contrast a "big city" and a "wilderness region" you might offer students these choices:

- Task 1 – Draw a region map of a wilderness area or a big city.
- Task 2 - Write a letter to a friend back home in the city describing your new life in the wilderness or your new life in a big city.

- Task 3 – Pretend you are a real estate agent and design a wilderness brochure that encourages people to move from the city.

- Task 4 – Develop a skit entitled "A Typical Day Where I Live."

A menu of tasks is a great tool for individualizing student learning, meeting special needs, and keeping all students engaged and interested. While the above example varied tasks based on different ways to present knowledge about a standard, you could also provide a menu of tasks based on difficulty level.

Guides on the Side

Having a menu is great, but it is also important that students understand what to do with an assignment. In other words, expectations need to be clear before the task is given. "Guides on the Side" provide students and parents with a student-friendly definition, maybe even an example, of good work before students begin the assignment. So, in addition to asking students to write a letter describing their first day in the wilderness or a big city, you could provide them with the following description of what a good letter should contain. You might even provide an example of a good letter. Here's an example of both.

Friendly Letter Guide on the Side Assignment: Write a letter to a friend back home telling them about your first day in the wilderness of North Carolina.

Guide on the Side:

- Time-sequenced and includes morning, lunch and evening activities

- Use descriptive language. Be sure to use all five senses as you describe the day to help the reader imagine it.

- Between 75-100 words

- No spelling errors

Sample of Proficient Work:

Dear T.J.,

Well we made it. The wagon didn't break down and we got to our new home in North Carolina. There are lots of trees and lakes. The wind blowing through the trees sounds just like the ocean back home.

My first day here I had to get up real early, while it was still dark, to take care of the animals. Guess what? Pigs are not slimy, but you were right. They do smell funny!

I went fishing after lunch and watched my granddad hunt squirrels. It got cold at night, so we played games and read close to the fire. I did not see a bear. Your friend,

Don

Figure 9 Guide on the Side Example

You might not include all these components, scenarios, menus, scoring guides and sample work all the time, but you can always try to include some of them. And your students can help you create all of these tools. See another example of an engaging scenario, multiple tasks and scoring guides in appendix A.

Chapter 6: Data

There are varying views on assessments – how to use them, whether they are useful, and whether students are over-tested. Some believe tests are evil and the people who defend them are trying to harm children and schools, while others believe tests are the only reliable information we have about student performance. What we are proposing is there is a genuine desire to get to the big question: What data do we need to improve teaching, leadership, and learning?

Big Tests and Little Tests

Often the backlash over testing is well deserved. In too many schools there are too many tests. We should not be surprised that accountability and teacher evaluation systems built around standardized tests caused schools to increase testing. The past several years we have had state achievement tests, graduation tests, the standardized tests, measures of academic readiness, dynamic indicators of literacy skills, end of quarter benchmark tests, end of course tests, college entrance tests, and all sorts of practice for the test tests.

How is all this testing impacting student achievement? Recent achievement data from NAEP (Nation's Report Card 2017), showed that 37% of fourth grade and 36% of eighth grade students scored at or above the proficient level on the reading assessment in 2017, which remains virtually the same as in 2015. Despite all the problems associated with testing, we are not going to suggest that standardized tests be expelled from schools. As public institutions under contract with their communities to help students learn, schools should be required to present evidence that they are doing their job. Standardized tests can provide part of that evidence and there is information we can gain from them. Standardized tests can help teachers, administrators and board members answer the questions at the end of the quarter or year:

- Did the students master the skills taught?
- Did our students master as many skills as students across the state or across the country?

These tests allow students' progress to be tracked over the years. For example, if a student scores in the 75th percentile in the sixth grade and the 86th percentile in the seventh grade, you can see that the child is gaining ground relative to grade-level peers. Administrators use big tests, like the Ohio Achievement Test or the Ohio Graduation Test to evaluate the effectiveness of curriculum, textbook and teachers.

Data Driven or Data Dizzy?

We can appreciate the need for assessing students, but we also argue against the assumption that tests alone provide sufficient information to improve instruction and increase student learning. Big tests are important, but they do not represent the full power of all types of assessments. Standardized tests allow us to look backwards and help us determine whether or not learning occurred, but the information is typically too much, too late and too vague to inform a teacher's day-to-day instruction. Teachers end up data-dizzy rather than data-driven. They'll say: What am I supposed to do? How should I change to make sure my students succeed? This test data tells me my students from last year scored low in math, but it doesn't give me anything specific to help me decide what and how to teach this group of students? The test reports showed that my students had trouble with fractions, but what specific skills are they missing? That is what I need to know. All the work our district does with test binders, action plans, and data walls seem to be more public relation than practical application.

Balanced Assessment: Classroom Assessments

The instructional decisions that have the greatest impact on student achievement are made by teachers not once a year when standardized test results roll in, but every few days. Well-designed classroom assessments could be an integral part of the assessment process. When incorporated into classroom practice, they could provide specific, personalized, and timely information about student misconceptions, student interests, and teacher misassumptions around specific skills.

The most effective classroom assessments measure students' skills and interests before instruction begins, immediately following instruction, and after teachers reteach what students did not learn the first time. First, before instruction, assessments help teachers design effective lessons by providing data regarding:

1. What students already know?

2. What students don't know?

3. How will I teach it?

Classroom assessments should not be painful to build, take or score. They should only have a handful of items and take about fifteen minutes to administer. Their purpose is to gather information about a student's readiness to learn the skills/standards taught in next week's lesson or the next unit. Teachers use the information to determine what needs to be taught, prerequisite skills students need, and grouping of students. For example, a student who demonstrates mastery of the geometry skill about to be taught can have the opportunity to engage in an enrichment activity while the other students learn the grade level geometry skill. Students scoring lower on the assessment would be provided skill-building activities to reach the necessary readiness level.

Next, and immediately following instruction, teachers assess whether students learned the skill. This assessment can be very similar to the pre-assessment, with a simple change of numbers or reading passages. The assessment, again, should be short so it does not take a long time to score. The teacher should be able to turn around and reteach within a few days of the assessment, so it cannot take a long time to grade.

Finally, teachers need to analyze the data and reteach based on what the data says. Reteaching can take place whole group or small group depending on need. For example, if 50% of students mastered RL.4.5 and 80% mastered RL.4.6, RL.4.5 would be retaught whole group, while RL.4.6 could be taught small group to the 20% that did not master the standard (see chart below).

| RL.4.5 | 50% Mastered | Reteach whole group |
| RL.4.6 | 80% Mastered | Reteach small group to only 20% that did not master |

The general rule is in the chart below. (Note: your school or county may have other guidelines on this, we would like you to follow their advice!)

75% and above	Small group reteaching
74% and below	Whole group reteaching

Reteaching standards do not need to be taught in lieu of new standards. Rather, blocks of time throughout the week can allow for teaching both, if scheduled carefully. After reteaching standards, they need to be assessed again. Assessing new standards can simply be 2 problems with RL.4.5 and RL.4.6 on the next assessment, in addition to the new standards taught that week.

Chapter 7: Teaching as a Team Sport

A leading educational researcher, Mike Schmoker (2006), believes there are two basic truths in education:

1. An effective teacher has more impact on student achievement than all other factors combined.

2. When teachers get together to talk in concrete, precise language about instruction and student work, their teaching dramatically improves, and student achievement rises

It is challenging for teachers to collaborate effectively together. Unfortunately, is the norm for teachers to work in isolation like independent contractors, sharing only the refrigerator and the parking lot. Each classroom is its own "microcosm." We recently surveyed 427 teachers in grades kindergarten through 12. The teachers were from public schools in Florida, Michigan and Ohio (Crouse, Amy & White, 2008). Here's what they told us about collaboration in their schools:

Teachers' Survey

In my opinion...	Strongly Disagree	Disagree	Agree	Strongly Agree	Don't Know
1. Instruction improves dramatically when teachers routinely get together to discuss assessment results and teaching strategies.	1%	10%	50%	35%	4%
2. I feel like I'm on my own when it comes to improving the achievement of my class.	7%	46%	33%	11%	3%
3. My instructional materials and practices match those of my grade level colleagues.	1%	18%	57%	12%	12%
4. Our current curriculum guide, calendar, or scope and sequence ensures that teachers are teaching the same thing at the same time.	4%	40%	43%	4%	9%
5. I would be thrilled if my son/daughter decided to become a teacher.	9%	34%	31%	11%	15%

Figure 10 Teachers' Survey

Even though eighty-five percent of the teachers thought collaboration improved instruction (Question 1), our remaining questions uncovered an alarming disconnect between knowing and doing. While teachers clearly understood collaboration was important, forty-four percent felt like they were "on their own" when it came to improving student achievement (Question 2). Nineteen percent of the surveyed teachers did not think their materials or instruction matched their same-grade colleagues, while another 12% were not sure (Question 3). And, nearly half of the teachers did not see their school's calendars, curriculum maps or scope & sequence charts helping their situation (Question 4). Perhaps it should not come as a surprise that almost half of our surveyed teachers would not like to see their own children become teachers. Why not? It could be because many teachers surveyed feel like teaching is a lonely profession (Question 5). Although the survey results are alarming, we do believe there is something that can be done about this problem. Great schools are able to meet together to talk about what is going well, what is not, and plans for improvement in their classrooms and on their grade levels.

Professional Learning Communities (PLC's) are…

As a principal twenty-five years ago at Adlai Stevenson High School in Illinois, Richard Dufour brought Professional Learning Communities (PLC's) to prominence (Dufour & Eaker, 1998). Small groups of teachers would meet weekly to create common formative assessments, analyze results, discuss strategies for improvement, and brainstorm creative units and lesson plans. These meetings focused on what was working with students, what wasn't working, and which students need extra help. Adlai Stevenson High School's name has appeared on the U.S. Department of Education's Blue-Ribbon list four times – an honor shared by only two other schools nationwide. Every year more than 3,000 educators visit the school to see PLC's in action. And today, professional learning communities, or as they are also called, data teams or team meetings, are thought to be the most promising strategy for improving instruction and student performance (Muhammad, 2018).

What makes these teams so powerful and empowering? It's this simple fact: You do not become a remarkable teacher alone. The journey is less about attaining perfection, but more about being a better teacher today than you were yesterday, about acknowledging imperfection and looking for competency and complementariness among your colleagues. PLC's allow you to magnify your strengths and work with other teachers that provide different but equally important strengths. So, the math teacher who is a master at number sense and data analysis may not be an expert on geometry. But the teacher across the hall cannot wait to share her engaging activity for scalene and isosceles triangles. While no single person will possess every dimension of an effective teacher, the team is likely to have many skills to complement each other. When teachers come together and talk about teaching, they realize that improvement is something they can generate, rather than something that is power pointed out to them by so-called experts.

~~~~~~

Successful PLCs in Practice

In my 18 years in public instruction, I have been a participant and a leader in two types of PLC meetings. At School A, teachers gather around a conference table after bathroom breaks and grabbing a snack. They casually talk about how their day is going and which students are particularly disruptive. They plan out their field trips, write parent letters, and grade papers not-so-secretly while others are talking. At some point they will pull up the lesson plans from last year and throw worksheets in the middle of the table to ask who needs which copies.

At School B, teachers enter within 5 minutes of start time (per the norms they created and posted on the wall), find their assigned seat at the table and check out their responsibility for the meeting. It could be that they are focusing on standards-alignment, aligning instruction to the upcoming assessment, analyzing exit tickets for each day, or simply taking notes on the shared agenda. Teachers come prepared with an outline of the plans already completed as pre-work. They share out their ideas and revise and adjust based on team feedback. They stand and model teaching one or two of the week's most demanding lessons for shared understanding and clarification. Each teacher leaves with a solid plan for the week's instruction.

~~~~~~

Teacher-Based Teams Are Not...

Sometimes schools think they have PLCs, but they lack the structure of School B in the story above. They'll get together and talk about assemblies, field trips, lunch duty and various "housekeeping" issues. These topics are important, but remember, real teacher work has to focus on: what's being taught, its relationship to standards, how students are learning and behaving, and what needs to be done to get all students to improve. Effective teacher teams are a group of teachers who believes they are collectively responsible for student success.

Organizational structures like PLC protocols are simply a way to structure the conversation, so all members participate, stay focused, and comply with group norms. Agendas that set time limits and topic boundaries can be especially helpful with hard-to-discuss topics by providing structure and psychological safety. And, they can come in handy if one or two members monopolize the discussion or elbow others out of the conversation. Forms and agendas can also help teams spell out ground rules and expectations for their work, including how consensus is defined, how conflicts will be resolved, how time will be spent. But they are not the real work, and if forms get in the way, change them or get rid of them!

How to Implement PLC Techniques

Developing a PLC, or at least a PLC attitude takes work and intentionality, and quite honestly, an initiative from the leaders in the school. It's unrealistic to think you can flip your school to PLC thinking overnight. Instead, take small steps that can start paving the way for active collaboration between teachers.

- Approach teachers whose skills you respect and ask them to observe your teaching and offer some suggestions on your methods.

- Ask to observe a teacher you respect. Say something as simple as, "I always hear students leaving your class still discussing what you taught. I'd love to see how you get that level of engagement. Do you mind if I sit in on one of your classes to observe?" or "I noticed your students mastered the indicator. What are you doing?"

- Ask colleagues about conferences or workshops that they've attended. Mention an article you've read that they may find interesting. Share a brochure on a workshop in another teacher's area of expertise.

- Don't think because you do not have a lot of years of experience that you have nothing to contribute. The flow of information doesn't always go from experienced teacher to new teacher. Just as you value the child in your class who asks pertinent questions, your questions are essential to the growth of you and your colleagues. Your questions encourage more experienced teachers to consider practices and the basis for them. You are also likely to hold the most current knowledge of cutting-edge educational research that can and should be discussed as well as well-developed information-gathering skills.

- Perhaps start with discussing student achievement on one common assessment. What did students do well? What did they struggle with? How can you reteach what they struggled with?

- If you are considering starting or reviving a PLC in your school, remember, simple plans work best. Here is a modest suggestion for activities your PLC could engage in:

What you might do:	Why you would do these things:
• Collaboratively score student work • Analyze student data on a standard • Identify lessons for remediation or enrichment • Adjust lessons • Share lesson ideas • Discuss consistent grading procedures	• Develop common understandings of what you are looking for • Pre-testing to plan instruction • Establish common rigor • Select exemplars • Support each other with planning

Simply put, if beginning a PLC to collaboratively discuss student data or planning, start small. Begin conversations that will lead to teachers discussing how students do on assessments and what to do about it. Just because you potentially do not have the years, does not mean you cannot begin the discussion!

Chapter 8: Self Care

We've been indoctrinated, particularly in the United States, with idea that the meaning of life should be found in work. Oren Cass (2018), the author of the book *The Once and Future Worker* writes "we tell people that their work should be their passion. 'Don't give up until you find a job that you love!' 'You should be changing the world!' we tell them." That is the message in commencement addresses, in pop culture, and in media.

It has also been ingrained in us to put everything we have into our jobs. As teachers, it is easy to literally take your work home with you, and figuratively as well. We often spend time worrying about our students when they are not with us or thinking about how we can serve them better. These are not bad traits, but we also want to express the importance of thinking of yourself as well! We encourage you to never feel like you need to give everything to your job, so much that you lose yourself. Or that you need to feel like you love every minute of your job. All jobs have long periods of stasis, boredom, busywork and work that we simply don't like. A mismatch between expectations and reality is a recipe for disappointment, if not outright misery.

People often enter teaching because they want to make a difference. They want to help students be the best they can be, as productive citizens. In this work, we have seen teachers put their own partners, children, and selves aside to help others. This often leads to burn out. According to Holme, Jabbar, Germain and Dinning (2018), some schools lose between one-third to one-half of their staff in single year. We equate the large turnover partially due to teachers becoming overwhelmed and not taking care of themselves first. This chapter has tips to make sure you are healthy, so you can then care for the students in your room.

Work/Life Balance

As a beginning teacher, there is much to do, and even if you went to a four-year university and student taught, there is nothing like your first year of teaching! You are attending meetings, maintaining a positive learning environment, learning new curriculum, planning engaging lessons, assessing, planning again, etc. It seems at times as if there is an endless amount of work to get done. At some point, you need to put that aside and do something that brings you joy.

Below are some suggestions for how to get the time that you need, and suggestions for doing so.

Plan the Time

It might sound silly, but you have to plan for the things that you really want. So, just like you plan for teaching, have a plan for personal time as well!

- Prioritize your time at work. Create a list of to-dos in the order in which they need to be completed. To-do lists might include planning, copies, grading, entering grades or other things assigned. Complete any tasks that are quick (only take minutes of your time) first. Then, complete tasks that are due the soonest next. NOTE: You may not complete all of the tasks on your to-do list, but that's ok! As long as the due date is not looming, save it for the next time!

- Once you have it, carve out time for your to-do list. Create a scheduled time each day for things on your list. You may be an early bird and enjoy working in the morning; arrive to school early, shut your door, and get your list done. Or, if you are an early start school, carve out an hour or two at the end of the day for your to-do list. Utilize any free planning you have for your list as well. Put this time on your schedule and stick to it.

- Leave one day a week to leave school early or arrive late.

- Do not leave for the day without being prepared for tomorrow. Set out handouts and student materials, arrange chairs and desks, and make sure presentation materials are ready.

- Be cautious of things that can be wasting your time. For example, is there a colleague that eats up 20 minutes of your planning complaining about her day? This might not be the best way to utilize your free time. Your time is extremely important, so do not waste it!

- Do not over-commit! Often times, counties, districts or schools will have rules (or at least recommendations) that beginning teachers do not have responsibilities beyond their required jobs (coach, leading the school play, run an after-school club, etc.) for good reason. Being a beginning teacher is hard work, and there is so much to learn your first few years. There are some things that are required, such as being on a school committee for example, and cannot be avoided. But, if you can, please do not overextend yourself because the outcome could be burnout!

Possible Schedule

This is a sample of what your schedule could look like. Time is broken up into before school, planning time, after school, and home. This schedule assumes there are meetings 3 days during planning, but not before or after school. Where there is NOTHING scheduled, that is time for you!

	Monday	Tuesday	Wednesday	Thursday	Friday
Before School	Prep for the Day To-Do List	Prep for the Day To-Do List	Prep for the Day To-Do List	Prep for the Day To-Do List	NOTHING
Planning	To-Do List	Meeting	Meeting	Meeting	To Do List
After School	Prep for Tomorrow	Prep for Tomorrow	Prep for Tomorrow	Prep for Tomorrow	NOTHING
Home	NOTHING	To do List	To do List	NOTHING	NOTHING

While we recognize Saturday or Sunday you may have to spend some time planning for the week, we hope you take a least one full day to rest, get some exercise or do something you enjoy. Not taking some time for yourself is a guarantee that burnout will be around the corner!

Figure 11 A suggested calendar of how to create a work/life balance

Play/Plan to Your Strengths

We all have unique strengths, and work should be one of the places we can express them and contribute them to the world. Yet only 2 out of 10 people say they use their strengths every day at work (Buckingham & Goodall, 2019).

1. Spend a week in love with your job. For one week, keep a "Loved it/Loathed it" list, and every time you look forward to a task or find time flying by during an activity, write it down in your "Loved It" column. Likewise, if you find yourself dragging your heels before a specific task, dreading it and slogging through it, write it down in the "Loathed It" column. By the end of the week you'll have a list of things that you love doing – these are strengthening activities for you – and will give you joy.

2. Now that you've identified your "red threads," the next thing to do is pull on them, weaving them deliberately into the fabric of your daily work. Look for – and seize – every opportunity to play to your strengths. 73% of people agree or strongly agree with the phrase "I have the opportunity to maneuver my job to fit my strengths better." That means it's likely that once you've identified your red threads at work, it is possible for you to find more ways to use them every day.

Find Joy Away from the Job

Once you have the time, use it to do things that bring you joy, excite you, or rejuvenate you. This could be spending time with a loved one, working out, knitting or spending time alone. Once you figure out the things that bring you joy, be sure to do them! Write them in your calendar so they become a priority (see Figure 11).

No matter what you do, remember that you are doing your very best at work, and can only continue to do so if you take care of yourself first. If you find that things become too overwhelming, or you are getting too stressed, make sure to reach out to someone, a professional, who can help you sort through how you're feeling. Your students need the very best of you, which you cannot give them if you are not well.

Conclusion

Becoming Remarkable

As we wrap up this book, we hope you have learned these long and lingering ideas:

- Remarkable teachers are reflective teachers.

- Open up, share and learn from your students, their parents and your colleagues.

- Expect great things from yourself, your students and the other players.

- Prioritize in order to find time for yourself.

There is nothing like your first few years of teaching. Improvement is slow – at first. Teachers and schools that move from poor to better or good to remarkable had no silver bullet program and didn't change overnight. Principals, consultants or books did not "motivate" teachers – their teachers were self-motivated. Remarkable teachers and schools aren't the result of a dramatic event. Instead, teachers that achieve great results hold high expectations for themselves and students, and commit to the long haul, knowing not every day is going to be perfect, but reflect each day and make the next better.

Cheers to jump-starting a great career!

Appendix A
Secret Agent Assignment

Here is an example of an engaging task that can be completed with upper elementary students. The assignment "Secret Agents" allows students to practice algebra concepts by coding and decoding messages. There are 5 leveled tasks starting with a basic task and moving up to an enrichment activity (along with scoring rubrics) for each task.

Grade Level: Upper Elementary

Topic: Students practice basic arithmetic and some pre-algebra operations by coding and decoding several messages.

Keywords:
Arithmetic operations
Code
Decode
Pre-algebra

Description

This assessment involves several levels of elementary math ability and introduces some pre-algebra concepts. Tasks 1 and 2 reinforce foundational arithmetic operations, while Tasks 3 and 4 require complex reasoning. For tasks 1 and 2, students should be encouraged to place lines between each number that represents a coded letter or <u>underline</u> each number that represents a letter. In addition, students should initially use a <u>symbol</u>, such as an *, &, ^, etc., as a <u>space</u> between words. You may want to provide the students with a template for them to use as a model.

Students who are ready for more advanced work can enrich Tasks 3 and 4 in several ways. First, they can use non-English languages to construct the messages to be sent. Second, they can use complex multi-step codes similar to those in Task 3. Third, they can use a computer spreadsheet to automatically encode and decode messages. Fourth, they can work with encoded messages of other students and attempt to decode them and determine the code rules the other students are using. Although these tasks can be accomplished with groups, each student must provide individual work to be evaluated.

If the students complete Tasks 1 through 4, enrichment tasks are provided at the end of the assessment. This adds an interesting angle to the assessment. An alphabet code sheet is provided at the end of the assessment for the students' use.

Required Materials

Information on codes needed for enrichment tasks
Code sheets
Optional: Templates for student's coded messages

Introduction

Secret agents have to communicate with each other using codes. Only people who know the code can understand what the messages mean. You will get to create your own messages, put them in a code, and decode the messages that your fellow secret agents send to you. If you do those jobs very well, your teacher may also ask you to create your own codes.

How do codes work? For this activity, a number represents each letter in the alphabet. For example, a simple code might look like this:

A = 1   B = 2   C = 3   D = 4

and so on.

But if a code is too easy, then the other secret agents can find out what is in your secret messages. Your codes are going to be more difficult, so that only you and your teammates know how to decode your messages.

Prepare for tasks: Get into groups

Task 1: Encode a message

Here are the steps you will follow:

- First, you will write your message. Make it at least two sentences long. You are going to give directions to the place someone will meet you. For example, your message might say:

  "Meet me at my house at three o'clock on Saturday. It's next to the bakery on Main Street."

- Next, put your message away and fill out a code sheet, showing what numbers are equal to which letters of the alphabet. Have a number for all 26 letters. Use the following coding rules to write out this code on the Alphabet Code Sheet.

  A = 2
  B = the value you used for A, multiplied by 2
  C = the value you used for A, multiplied by 3
  D = the value you used for A, multiplied by 4

  and so on. You also need code numbers or symbols for spaces between words, and for numbers that you might use in addresses or phone numbers. Remember that you cannot use a number that has already been used for your letters. Write your code list on the Alphabet Code Sheet, and label it "Task 1." Stop and have one of your partners check your work. Make sure that your code numbers are right!

- Now you have the message you wrote and you have your code sheet. Change your message into numbers using this code. Write your coded message; use only numbers.

- Give JUST the coded message to one of your partners. Let him or her try to decode the message. Then see if he or she got it right.

- If your partner doesn't get the message decoded, see if you can figure out where the mistake is. DON'T do the decoding for your partner – just see if you can find the mistake. Write a note to your partner explaining why you think he or she got it wrong. If your partner figured out the code, write that down.

- Everyone in the group should have these five things to show the teacher:
  1) your original message, written in words
  2) your Alphabet Code List that shows all the letters and shows which code numbers go with each letter
  3) your encoded message, that looks like a number sentence
  4) your partner's effort to decode your message

5) your note to your partner

Task 1 Scoring Guide

4   Exemplary

❑ Criteria for the Proficient category have been successfully completed.
❑ More advanced work is completed. For example, the student recognizes the pattern in the code rule and explains it. The student explains how he or she decided on the numbers used for spaces and address numbers. Other examples of advanced work include:

_____

3   Proficient

❑ The message is at least two sentences long.
❑ The meaning of the message is clear and doesn't use any tricks.
❑ There are no spelling errors in the sentences.
❑ The numbers for each letter of the alphabet are correctly calculated.
❑ The partner's decoding is included.
❑ A note to the partner tells whether he or she figured out the code correctly, and tells what the error is, if any.

_____

2   Progressing

❑ Four or five of the criteria in the Proficient category have been met.
❑ More work is needed.

_____

1   Not meeting the standard(s)

❑ Less than four of the criteria in the Proficient category have been met.
❑ The task should be repeated.

Task 2: Make up your own code

Now that you know how to use a secret agent code, it's time to write your own code.

Use these steps:

- First, write the math rule that you will use to create your code. For example,

A = 2	D = C x 3	G = F x 2
B = A x 3	E = D x 2	
C = B x 2	F = E x 3	

  and so on. Create any rule you want – and remember to keep it a secret from your fellow secret agents! Write the rule down on a piece of paper. Also write the code list on the Alphabet Code Sheet and label this "Task 2."

- Using words write a **message** with at least two sentences.

- Put the message in code. Write your message and your coded message on separate pieces on paper.

- Give JUST the coded message to one of your partners. Allow him or her to decode the message. Then see if he or she got it right.

- If your partner doesn't get the message decoded, see if you can figure out where the mistake is. DON'T do the decoding for your partner – just see if you can find the mistake. Write a note to your partner explaining why you think he or she got it wrong. If your partner figured out the code, write that down.

- Everyone in the group should have these five things to show the teacher:

  1) your original message
  2) your coding rule and your alphabet code list showing all the letters and numbers, and which code numbers go with each letter
  3) your encoded message
  4) your partner's effort to decode your message
  5) your note to your partner

Task 2 Scoring Guide

4   Exemplary

- ❑ Criteria for the Proficient category have been successfully completed.
- ❑ Advanced work is completed. For example, the student uses at least two arithmetic operations to encode the message. The student identifies and explains the numerical pattern in his or her code. Other examples of advanced work include:

---

3   Proficient

- ❑ The coding rule uses one arithmetic operation.
- ❑ The message is at least two sentences long. The meaning of the message is clear and doesn't use any tricks. There are no spelling errors in the sentences.
- ❑ The numbers for each letter of the alphabet (code list) are correctly calculated. The partner's decoding is included.
- ❑ A note to the partner tells whether he or she figured out the code correctly, and tells what the error is, if any.

---

2   Progressing

- ❑ Three of the criteria in the Proficient category have been met.
- ❑ More work is needed.

---

1   Not meeting the standard(s)

- ❑ Less than three of the criteria in the Proficient category have been met.
- ❑ The task should be repeated

If you need to do some more work on the first two tasks, that's OK. It's important to understand how to use the math rule to get the codes and how to use them to make codes. Your teacher might ask you to do these tasks again. Only go on to the next task if your teacher says that it's OK.

Task 3: Make another code

Here is what you will do: You are going to write codes again, but this time you have to give directions to another secret agent using a map. You can choose any map you want – city, state, national, or world map. In your message, describe where you want the secret agent to go. He or she is starting at your school. You have to tell him or her how many miles or kilometers to go, and in what direction to travel. For example, your message might say, "Meet me in New York City. From our town, you have to travel 2,380 miles to the east." Decide on what measurement you will use. Use your map and the scale on the map to determine the direction and distance you will use in your message.

Here are the specific steps you need to follow:

- Create your own **code** but use a different code than you did earlier in this activity. First, write the math rule that you will use to create your code. For example, A = 2, then B = A x 3, and so on. Create any rule you want – and remember to keep it a secret from your partners! Only you know the code.

- Write down the **rule** on a piece of paper. Now write the code list on an Alphabet Code Sheet and label it "Task 3."

- Using letters, write a **message** that has clear and accurate directions – remember to use both direction and distance in your message.

- Put this message into code. Write your message and your coded message on separate pieces of paper.

- Give your coded message to one of your partners. See if he or she can decode the message. If the message is not decoded, see if you can figure out where the mistake is. DON'T do the decoding for your partner – just see if you can find the mistake. Write a note to your partner explaining why you think he or she got it wrong. If your partner figured out the code, write that down.

- Everyone in the group should have these five things to show the teacher:

  1) your original message, along with the map that you used for your directions
  2) your coding rule and your alphabet code list showing all the letters and numbers, and which code numbers go with each letter
  3) your encoded message
  4) your partner's effort to decode your message
  5) the note to your partner

Task 3 Scoring Guide

4   Exemplary

❑ Criteria for the Proficient category have been successfully completed.
❑ More advanced work is included. For example, the work clearly explains the relationship of the scale to the distance described in the message. The coding rule uses at least two arithmetic operations. Other examples of advanced work include:

---

3   Proficient

❑ The distance and directions are accurate.
❑ The coding rule uses at least one arithmetic operation.
❑ The message is at least two sentences long and has no errors.
❑ The code list is completely accurate.
❑ The partner's decoding is included, and the student accurately evaluates whether or not the decoding is correct.

---

2   Progressing

❑ Four of the criteria in the Proficient category have been met.
❑ More work is needed.

---

1   Not meeting the standard(s)

❑ Less than four of the criteria in the Proficient category have been met.
❑ The task should be repeated.

Only go on to the next task if your teacher says that it's OK.

Task 4: Harder codes with multi-steps

The problem with some secret agent codes is that the other secret agents are just as smart as you are! That means that the best secret agents always have to invent codes that are hard for other agents to decode.

You have already done "single-step" codes. In those codes, each letter was the same as one number. Now you are going to figure out a more complicated code system, where each code will require more steps. If you know about more advanced math operations, such as exponents, this is a good time to use them. Remember, the more complicated your message, the harder it will be for the other agents to figure it out!

How do you make a "multi-step" code? The rule that you write has to have more than one step for each letter. In addition, the code might change from day to day. For example:

> A = today's day of the month. For example, if today were October 3rd, A would be equal to 3.

> B = A^2 in this example, B would be equal to 3 x 3 or 9.

> C = $A^2 + 1$

> D = $A^2 + 2$, and so on.

> Remember that the value of these letters would change with every day. For example, on October 4th, A would be equal to 4.

In this problem, you're going to give directions again. This time you don't know if the other secret agent knows about the metric system, so you're going to have given directions in both miles **and** kilometers.

Here are the steps you need to follow:

- Write down the **rule** on a piece of paper. Now write the code list on an Alphabet Code Sheet and label it "Task 4."

- Write a **message** that has clear and accurate directions. Remember to use both direction and distance in your message, and then put the message in code. Write your message and your coded message on separate pieces of paper.

- Now give your coded message to one of your partners. See if he or she can decode the message. If the message isn't decoded, see if you can figure out where the mistake is. DON'T do the decoding for your partner – just see if you can find the mistake. Write a note

87

to your partner explaining why you think he or she got it wrong. If your partner figured out the code, write that down.

- Everyone in the group should have these five things to show the teacher:

  1) your original message, along with the map that you used for your directions (both miles and kilometers)
  2) your coding rule and your alphabet code list showing all the letters and numbers, and which code numbers go with each letter
  3) your encoded message
  4) your partner's effort to decode your message
  5) the note to your partner

Task 4 Scoring Guide

4   Exemplary

❑ Criteria for the Proficient category have been successfully completed.
❑ More advanced work is included. For example, the work clearly shows the relationship of the scale to the distance described in the message. The coding rule uses at least two arithmetic operations. Other examples of advanced work include:

---

3   Proficient

❑ The distance and directions are accurate.
❑ The coding rule uses at least one arithmetic operation that is different from the earlier tasks.
❑ The message is at least two sentences long.
❑ The meaning is understandable.
❑ The words are spelled correctly.
❑ The code list is completely accurate.
❑ The partner's decoding is included, and the student accurately evaluates whether or not the decoding is correct.

---

2   Progressing

❑ Five or six of the criteria in the Proficient category have been met.
❑ More work is needed.

---

1   Not meeting the standard(s)
❑ Less than five of the criteria in the Proficient category have been met.
❑ The task should be repeated.

Enrichment Tasks

If you completed all four tasks and you would like some additional interesting work about codes, talk with your teacher about the following ideas:

1) Use a computer spreadsheet to make your code list, and automatically encode and decode messages.

2) Read more about the use of codes by secret agents. Many important events in history, including the development of the atom bomb, the Civil War, and the German attacks on England were all at the center of fascinating stories about the use of codes by secret agents.

3) Take some of the codes that your classmates have developed and look JUST at the coded numbers – NOT at the code list. Working JUST with the coded numbers; try to figure out what the message is and what the math rule is.

4) Write a story about the use of codes as a secret agent. Use some of your coded messages as part of the story.

5) What about real codes today? The CIA won't just tell you what they are! But real codes are sometimes also based on time. That is, at 10:02, A=2, but at 10:03, A=4. Both you and person receiving the code have to have very, very accurate clocks for this to work. Can you develop a code like this?

Alphabet Code Sheet

Your name_____

Task name or number_____

Letter	Code No. 1 Code value	Rule	Code No. 2 Code value	Rule
A				
B				
C				
D				
E				
F				
G				
H				
I				
J				
K				
L				
M				
N				
O				
P				
Q				
R				
S				
T				
U				
V				
W				
X				
Y				
Z				

Appendix B
Resources

This appendix contains all of the resources (checklists, tips, tables, etc.) by chapter from this text.

We hope that having all of these in one place will make it easier to access year after year.

Chapter 1 Resources

Personality Test Links

- Meyers-Briggs - https://www.16personalities.com/free-personality-test

- Enneagram - https://tests.enneagraminstitute.com/

Tips for Introductory Parent Phone Calls

- Before going into conversations with parents, be prepared with questions to ask, information you would like to share with them, and answers to typically asked questions (see below)

- Take notes as you talk with them (see below)

Questions for Parents/Guardians

- What do you feel is the most important thing for me to know about your child?

- Who are the important people in your child's life?

- How does your child learn best?

- Is there anything else I need to know about your child?

Information you May Want to Share

**A word of caution first, do not share personal information with students, parents or guardians. There is a difference between telling a little about yourself to build relationships and oversharing. Check with a mentor or coach if you need support with these conversations.

- A little about yourself (we do not suggest you start off telling them this is your first-year teaching)
- Teaching style or philosophy
- What a typical day looks like for their child
- Discipline policy
- Communication (how best to get ahold of you and when you will respond) It is critical to establish mutual expectation around the type and frequency of communication.

Typically Asked Questions

- What is the policy on late work?
- How are differences in learning accommodated?
- What is the discipline policy?
- How will I know if my child is performing on grade level?
- Is there a gifted program and how do I get into it?
- How can I get my child extra help if they do not understand something?
- How can I help my child at home?

Parent Phone Call Log

Date	Time	Placed by	Name of Parent	Child's Name & Reason for Call	Notes

Tips for if a Parent is Upset

- First, remember, as stated above, almost all parents are coming from a place of love for their child.

- Allow the parent to voice their concern.

- Do not get into a situation where you are emailing back and forth with a parent. It is often better to discuss their concern in person, rather than through email or on the phone.

- If necessary, have a mentor, curriculum support person, assistant principal, or principal present when talking with the parent.

- When the parent expresses his or her concern, do not react emotionally; rather, state the facts of the situation and allow those to lead the conversation, instead of emotion.

- Come to the table with solutions for the issue.

- Confirm understanding and acceptance. "Mrs. Sanders, do you agree this is a good plan for our next step?"

- Leave the conversation with a plan to help their child that both parties can live with.

- Plan a follow up, whether through email, phone call or in person.

Classroom Newsletters

- important upcoming events in the classroom and school

- dates to remember

- curriculum notes and current topics of study

- materials needed in the classroom or a wish list

- changes to class rules or policies

- details about field trips

- informational surveys

- messages of thanks for materials or to volunteers

- ideas to help parents support kids at home

- ways for parents to be involved (Parents have varying degrees of comfort in helping their students. Offer easy and concrete ways parents can support student success through everyday activities.)

- photos of recent activities

- congratulations to students for achievements

- requests for volunteer support – remember to include ways for working parents to help you. Are there donated items that you need – scrap paper? Discarded binders? Baby food jars? Parents who support your classroom will be more invested in the collective success of your classroom – Make every parent feel as if they have something to offer your class that will be beneficial to student outcomes

Chapter 2 Resources

Student Questionnaires

- Beginning of Year Questionnaire: https://pernillesripp.com/2013/07/23/my-student-questionnaire-for-beginning-of-year/

- First day of school questionnaire: https://www.csun.edu/science/ref/management/student-questionnaire/student-questionnaires.html

- What Kids Can Do Questionnaire:

  http://www.whatkidscando.org/specialcollections/student_voice/pdf/Who%20Are%20You%20Questionnaire.PDF

Tips for Delivering Questionnaires

- Consider giving each student a small journal and some old magazines and see what they value. They can paste pictures of their interests and date that page. They can add to the journal as their interests grow and evolve throughout the year.

- Have students interview one another and introduce themselves to you.

- Have students bring in pictures of people that are important to them.

- Have them write poetry or songs.

Morning Meeting Ideas

- Get to know you activities

- Exciting things that happened the night/day before

- Content or data review

- Energizers

- Reminders for the day

Information About Students' Academics

- Review student cumulative records to gather data about your students as learners. Look at all academic records.

- Analyze state test data to identify strengths and weaknesses in individual students and the class as a whole.

- Ask to see a copy of your school's state report card and find out if your state offers on-line reports such as item analyses and individual student reports.

- Look for a folder containing an Individualized Educational Plan (IEP).

- Make an appointment with the special education teacher in your building to review the IEP goals of your students and discuss how you will work together to help them achieve these goals.

Ideas for Getting to Know Your Students

- Ideas for getting to know your students

- Tour the neighborhood they live in

- Develop/borrow a questionnaire (see examples in this chapter)

- Have students bring pictures (or draw pictures) of people that are important to them

- Have students create connections to each other by sitting in a circle and saying one thing that is unique about them. If someone connects with that in some way, they throw a ball of yarn to that person. When they are done, they see the web they have created that shows the connections they have to each other.

- Have students create an inner circle and outer circle. Ask a question to the students and have them each answer, then the inside circle rotates, and another question is asked.

- Take time to know how to spell and pronounce each child's name correctly.

- Implement a short morning meeting into your schedule each morning.

- Take time to review their cumulative folders at the beginning of each school year.

Chapter 3 Resources

Checklist of Routines

Things that may need a routine:

- Getting students attention (attention getter)

- Entry Routine (when students enter classroom)

    - Where to sit

    - What to unpack

    - Where to put coat, book bag, homework

    - What to do when done unpacking (bell ringer)

- Transitions

    - Tables to carpet

    - Carpet to tables

    - Tables to line up

    - Carpet to line up

    - Outside the classroom to desks

    - Outside the classroom to carpet

- Attendance

- Lunch count

- Materials (how to get and how to put away)

- Distributing papers

- Collecting homework

- Collecting in class work

- What to do when finished with an assignment

- Sharpening pencils

- Getting a tissue

- Getting technology such as iPads or chrome books

- Rotating during centers (practice each rotation without actually having students do work)

Tips and Tricks for Developing Routines

- Develop a plan for routines

- If possible, physically sit in students' seat or stand in classroom when planning

- Practice the plan over and over

- Review after long breaks

- Utilize table or class helpers to speed up routines

- When student behavior is getting under your skin, ask yourself "do I have a routine for that, and have I taught it to my students"

- Make anchor charts of important routines and post around the classroom at the beginning of the year

- Practice what not to do to avoid common mistakes

Chapter 4 Resources

Possible "Time Wasters"

- Transitions from or to lunch, specials, bathroom

- Transitions inside the classroom (i.e. passing out papers, sharpening pencils)

- Beginning of class

- End of class

- Prepping materials for the day (pulling up slide shows, getting materials for the students, etc.)

- Time in between activities in class

Tips for Making a Schedule

- Chunk blocks of time so you are not doing direct instruction for long periods of time, no matter what the grade level. (Note: One thing I tell my teachers is take a student's age and add one. That is usually how long they can be sitting in one task)

- Consider transition times to and from periods, and in between activities. This time should not be long. I know Kindergarteners that can move from one place to another in seconds, especially if the teacher is counting down (this seems like a game and is fun for them).

- While it doesn't need to be posted, develop a plan for your planning time. Some time will be devoted to grade level meetings but be sure to have a plan for "free" planning times to maximize your productivity.

Developing a Pacing Calendar

- Know your standards. Typically, these can be found online or ask your mentor.

- Consider when your final assessments are, whether the students are taking end of course or end of year assessments. Put those on the calendar.

- Give yourself some review days (maybe a week or so depending on the course) before the final assessment. Put those on the calendar.

- Consider when it might make the most sense to teach the standards. For example, you may have quarterly assessments where you need to cover a certain number of standards. You would then want to make sure all of those standards are taught before the assessment. Differently, you may have standards that build upon one another, so they make sense to be taught in a certain order.

- Finally, calendar out your standards, and make sure there are no standards missing.

Planning Units

- First, think about your unit assessment. What standards do students need to know? How are you going to assess them? Create your assessment, schedule your assessment day, and perhaps a review day before the assessment.

- Then, how much time will you need for each standard? Consider how you are going to teach each standard and how much time you will need. Standards are typically complex and have multiple parts that need to be broken up. How will you break those up into lessons and how many days will you need?

- Finally, plan each day. Think about how your block will be broken up and how you will teach students something, but also have them practice.

- Reflection is also important. On your day-to-day calendar, choose one with space to record ideas for reflection and improving yesterday's lesson.

- Also, on your day-to-day calendar, record school-wide events, test days, appointments with school personal, and other personal appointments, and anything else that you need to remember. Make a habit of checking your calendar each day as often as is appropriate.

Preparing a Substitute Folder

- Provide detailed lesson plans for the sub. Fill your substitute folder with meaningful activities that can be done at any time during the year. For example, a Time for Kids magazine with a lesson to practice determining importance within non-fiction text, or a math and science graphing activity involving classroom materials that are always on hand.

- Make sure your sub knows how to log into your computer and other technology devices. Often, schools will provide a substitute login. Do not give substitutes your log in, as they may be able to access information they should not have.

- Have a folder with a seating chart and explanation of classroom procedures. Provide enough detail about procedures so the substitute can flawlessly run the class, including transitions, how students get and organize materials, where they turn in materials, etc.

- Designate a colleague who knows your classroom to be a backup for unforeseen circumstances and offer to do the same for him or her. Provide the name of this colleague to your sub as well as how they can help.

- Also provide names of student assistants who can support the sub in the classroom.

- In the beginning of the year, explain your expectations for students' appropriate interaction with a substitute. Then, if you know you will be absent, remind them again.

Chapter 5 Resources

Fostering Emotional Engagement

- Meet students at the door in the morning. Genuinely be interested about their evening, morning, etc.

- Take pictures of the students working and display them.

- Use humor but not sarcasm

- Use words, songs, or dances from students' lives. Teach them about these things from your life as well.

- Volunteer to serve as a sponsor, advisor or chaperone to after-school clubs, organizations and events.

- Compliment students on what they are wearing.

- Make a point of watching at least one television program that your students watch.

- Be aware of video games they are playing and their music and Internet culture.

Engaging Scenarios

Elementary

- You've been asked to design a new Nintendo Game…

- You are on the committee to help our principal revise spirit week with new themes…

- As crime scene investigators, we need determine who borrowed our…

- Develop a movie script that is about searching for…

- A famous author wants you to write a different ending to his/her book…

Middle School

- Your community is considering a teen curfew. Write a letter to the editor of the local newspaper…

- Some of the surrounding schools are switching to a school uniform policy…

- Design a game that teaches young students…

- Make a timeline that shows the history of…

- Develop a song lyric that describes your…

High School

- As a member of the Senate, make the case for or against allowing kids to vote at seventeen…

- You are trying to help your older brother decide if it's better to rent or buy a house…

- Write a report that describes working with…

- Draw a picture that will get students interested in…

- Develop a concept map that will help your classmates…

Chapter 7 Resources

Implementing PLCs

- Approach teachers whose skills you respect and ask them to observe your teaching and offer some suggestions on your methods.

- Ask to observe a teacher you respect. Say something as simple as, "I always hear students leaving your class still discussing what you taught. I'd love to see how you get that level of engagement. Do you mind if I sit in on one of your classes to observe?" or "I noticed your students mastered the indicator. What are you doing?"

- Ask colleagues about conferences or workshops that they've attended. Mention an article you've read that they may find interesting. Share a brochure on a workshop in another teacher's area of expertise.

- Don't think because you do not have a lot of years of experience that you have nothing to contribute. The flow of information doesn't always go from experienced teacher to new teacher. Just as you value the child in your class who asks pertinent questions, your questions are essential to the growth of you and your colleagues. Your questions encourage more experienced teachers to consider practices and the basis for them. You are also likely to hold the most current knowledge of cutting-edge educational research that can and should be discussed as well as well-developed information-gathering skills.

- Perhaps start with discussing student achievement on one common assessment. What did students do well? What did they struggle with? How can you reteach what they struggled with?

- If you are considering starting or reviving a PLC in your school, remember, simple plans work best. Here is a modest suggestion for activities your PLC could engage in:

What you might do:	Why you would do these things:
- Collaboratively score student work	- Develop common understandings of what you are looking for
- Analyze student data on a standard	
- Identify lessons for remediation or enrichment	- Pre-testing to plan instruction
- Adjust lessons	- Establish common rigor
- Share lesson ideas	- Select exemplars
- Discuss consistent grading procedures	- Support each other with planning

Chapter 8 Resources

Planning for Self-Care

- Prioritize your time at work! Create a list of to-dos in the order in which they need to be completed. To-do lists might include planning, copies, grading, entering grades or other things assigned. Complete any tasks that are quick (only take minutes of your time) first. Then, complete tasks that are due the soonest next. NOTE: You may not complete all of the tasks on your to-do list, but that's ok! As long as the due date is not looming, save it for the next time!

- Once you have it, carve out time for your to-do list. Create a scheduled time each day for things on your list. You may be an early bird and enjoy working in the morning; arrive to school early, shut your door, and get your list done. Or, if you are an early start school, carve out an hour or two at the end of the day for your to-do list. Utilize any free planning you have for your list as well. Put this time on your schedule and stick to it.

- Leave one day a week to leave school early or arrive late.

- Do not leave for the day without being prepared for tomorrow. Set out handouts and student materials, arrange chairs and desks, and make sure presentation materials are ready.

- Be cautious of things that can be wasting your time. For example, is there a colleague that eats up 20 minutes of your planning complaining about her day? This might not be the best way to utilize your free time. Your time is extremely important, so do not waste it!

- Do not over-commit! Often times, counties, districts or schools will have rules (or at least recommendations) that beginning teachers do not have responsibilities beyond their required jobs (coach, leading the school play, run an after-school club, etc.) for good reason! Being a beginning teacher is hard work, and there is so much to learn your first few years. There are some things that are required, such as being on a school committee for example, and cannot be avoided. But, if you can, please do not overextend yourself because the outcome could be burnout!

Possible Schedule

This is a sample of what your schedule could look like. Time is broken up into before school, planning time, after school, and home. This schedule assumes there are meetings 3 days during planning, but not before or after school. Where there is NOTHING scheduled, that is time for you!

	Monday	Tuesday	Wednesday	Thursday	Friday
Before School	Prep for the Day To-Do List	Prep for the Day To-Do List	Prep for the Day To-Do List	Prep for the Day To-Do List	NOTHING
Planning	To-Do List	Meeting	Meeting	Meeting	To Do List
After School	Prep for Tomorrow	Prep for Tomorrow	Prep for Tomorrow	Prep for Tomorrow	NOTHING
Home	NOTHING	To do List	To do List	NOTHING	NOTHING

While we recognize Saturday or Sunday you may have to spend some time planning for the week, we hope you take a least one full day to rest, get some exercise or do something you enjoy. Not taking some time for yourself is a guarantee that burnout will be around the corner!

References

Aguilar, E. (2018). *Onward: Cultivating Emotional Resilience in Educators*. San Francisco, CA: Jossey-Bass.

Buckingham, M. & Goodall, A. (2019). *Nine Lies About Work: A Freethinking Leader's Guide to the Real World of Work*. Boston, MA: Harvard Business Review Press.

Burgess, D. (2012). *Teach Like a Pirate*. San Diego, CA: Dave Burgess Consulting.

Cass, O. (2018). *The Once and Future Worker*. New York, NY: Encounter Books.

Coleman, J. S., Campbell, E. Q., Hobson, C. J., McPartland, J., Mood, A. M., Weinfeld, F. D., and York, R. L. (1966). *Equality of educational opportunity*. Washington, DC: U.S. Government Printing Office.

Dufour, R. & Eaker, R. (1998). *Professional Learning Communities at Work*. Bloomington, IN: National Education Service.

Goleman, D., Boyatzis, R., & McKee, A. (2002). *Primal leadership: Realizing the power of emotional intelligence*. Boston: Harvard Business School Press.

Holme, J. Jabbar, H. Germain, E. (2018). *Rethinking Teacher Turnover: Longitudinal Measures of Instability in Schools*. Educational Researcher, Oct. 2017, Vol. 47, 62-75.

Hurr, N. (2007). Student first-day of school questionnaires. Retrieved from https://www.csun.edu/science/ref/management/student-questionnaire/student-questionnaires.html

Inman, D., & Marlow, L. (2004). Teacher retention: Why do beginning teachers remain in the profession? *Education, 124*(4), 605-614.

Kohn, Alfie (1999). *The Schools Our Children Deserve: Moving Beyond Traditional Classroom and Tougher Standards*. New York, NY: Houghton Mifflin Company.

Lamb, Bri. (2019). Teacher's back-to-school 'baggage' activity goes viral for all the right reasons. Retrieved from https://foreverymom.com/society/inspiration/viral-back-to-school-baggage-activity/.

Marzano, Robert J. (2007). *The Art and Science of Teaching; A Comprehensive Framework for Effective Instruction.* Alexandria, VA: Association for Supervision and Curriculum Development.

Morse, G. (2005, June). *Hidden harassment.* Harvard Business Review, 28-30.

Muhammad, A. (2017). *Transforming School Culture: How to Overcome Staff Division. Bloomington.* IN: Solution Tree.

Ripp, P. (2013, July 23). *My student questionnaire for beginning of year.* Retrieved from https://pernillesripp.com/2013/07/23/my-student-questionnaire-for-beginning-of-year/

Rogers, S. (2013). *Teaching for Excellence.* Golden, CO: Peak Learning Systems, Inc.

Scott, E. (2019, August 27). *Teacher introduces powerful 'baggage activity' for the first day back to school.* Retrieved from https://metro.co.uk/2019/08/27/teacher-introduces-powerful-baggage-activity-first-day-back-school-10637562/

Sixteen Personalities. (2011-2019). Retrieved from https://www.16personalities.com/free-personality-test

Templeton, B. L. (2011). *Understanding Poverty in the Classroom.* Lanham, MD: Rowman & Littlefield Publishers

The Education Trust. (2019). Dispelling the myth. Retrieved from https://edtrust.org/dispelling_the_myth/

The Enneagram Institute. (2017). Retrieved from https://tests.enneagraminstitute.com/

What Kids Can Do. (2012). Retrieved from http://www.whatkidscando.org/specialcollections/student_voice/pdf/Who%20Are%20You%20Questionnaire.PDF

Wong, H. K. & Wong, R. T. (2018). *The First Days of School* (5th ed). Mountain View, CA: Harry K. Wong Publications, Inc.

Zhao, Y. (2010). Preparing globally competent teachers: A new imperative for teacher education. *Journal of Teacher Education, 61*(5), 422-431. https://doi.org/10.1177/0022487110375802